A Whisper From Your Soul™

Hear what you _really_ need to hear...

© 2012 God c/o A. Drayton Boylston

Also by A. Drayton Boylston

- <u>Coming UnScrooged</u>! A Contemporary Classic of Corporate Rescue and Redemption

- <u>The Sage and Scholars Guide to Coaching Executives</u>

- The Leadership Lantern

- <u>Rescued Executive Series</u>:
    - Coach as Lifeguard
    - Executive CPR
    - Coach as EMT

- A Short Guide to Corporate Rescue

- Exploring Coaching
  (Co-author Will Craig)

To sign up for A Whisper From Your Soul email program <u>click here</u>.

To gain additional insights, please go to the website: <u>www.rescueinstitute.org</u>

Publishers Cataloging-in-Publication Data

Boylston, A. Drayton.

A Whisper From Your Soul- Hear what you really need to hear.

/ A. Drayton Boylston.—Golden, Colo.: Rescue Institute Publishing, 2012.

p. ; cm.

ISBN-13: 978-0-9749314-0-1

ISBN-10: 0-9749314-0-3

1. Personal Development—United States—Fiction. 2. Corporate Culture—United States—Fiction. 3. Organizational Change—United States—Fiction.

I. Title.

PS3602.0957 C66   2006

813.6—dc22   0603

Interior Design & Composition: Jessfer Comendador

Edited by Jennifer-Crystal Johnson
www.jennifercrystaljohnson.com

Printed in the U.S.A.

First Edition

HB Printing 10 9 8 7 6 5 4 3 2 1

Please visit our websites:

www.WhisperFromYourSoul.com

www.RescueInstitute.com

www.ExecutiveCoachingUniversity.com

Please call for bulk purchase discounts: 1.800.251.1696.

Table of Contents

Forward: Why the Whispers?

Like many wonderful things, this started as something that I was putting great resistance up around. It was my initial foray into Twitter and I thought I must be crazy to even entertain this social vortex time sponge. I had been coerced ☺ by one of my colleagues to give it a shot. Begrudgingly, I did. Boy, am I glad I listened…

You see, my first challenge was- "What in the world was I going to say in 140 characters or less." My first thought was: there is no way I'm going to ramble on about what I was doing or where I was. I just couldn't. As I began to look at what was being Tweeted (yep, I've even embraced the jargon) I realized that there was a void. There wasn't anyone without a real agenda that was looking to serve others with their posts. Most of what I was seeing was overt selling and/or things that I didn't see much inherent value in for those reading the posts.

So, I began to write…and write I did…

It really felt like I was journaling- on a massive scale. The thoughts just poured from me (as divine inspiration always does when it flows from a person). I found myself not only embracing the enforced brevity requirement of the posts but reveling in the simplicity and purity of the messages that were being given to me. As usually happens when I get inspired, and especially when I write, I simply feel like a conduit. It is not from me but from a place that knows so much more than I ever will. These messages simply came *through* me.

How did I know this? I sat down one weekend and wrote down over 300 messages. Try doing *that* with no inspiration! Clearly, there is no way I could have done anything like this without divine inspiration. I literally could not type fast enough to capture them as fast as they were emerging.

Hence, I can't take credit for the copyright for these. Only He (or She, or Spirit, or The Divine- whichever works for you) can…

I took these messages and started posting them as Tweets. Much to my amazement people started retweeting them (sending them along to their "followers"). I started to get all these notifications that my tweets were spreading around cyberspace at an amazing pace. My Twitter account soon had thousands of followers. My Tweets were soon being sent to hundreds of thousands of people on a daily basis.

I was just blown away!

I then discovered that my Tweets had risen to the top 1.5% of all Tweets for the amount of retweets we were being blessed with. Clearly, these messages were resonating with many folks across the world.

And that led me to this book…

I felt compelled to make a compilation of these messages so people could read them in a more traditional fashion- in book form. I've designed this book as a Daily Devotional but it certainly can be read in one sitting or accessed in any way you deem appropriate. I'm not attached to any particular approach. I simply know that I have been prompted to share these.

Personal confession here: It has been a (heretofore undiscovered) calling of mine to pen a Daily Devotional and I didn't know it until recently.

I'm always amazed at how teachers show up in our lives. One of my biggest teachers was my mom. She was a true divine spirit and blessed me with many great lessons and values. Each year of my life from my teen years on, she would give me a daily devotional book every Christmas and she would inscribe them with the most beautiful and inspiriting words. I treasured each and every one. As I write this I still have one (God Calling) on my bedside table that I am reading for the 4th time. Little did she know (or did she? ☺) what all of the seeds she was planting would turn into. I certainly didn't- until now.

So here we are with these simple words that became thoughts which I wish to share with you. My desire is that you find peace, guidance, and anything else you may let emerge as you read these.

As you read each page take some time to write down whatever thoughts come up for you, let them simply emerge; they may feel random, off topic, or maybe even a bit bizarre. Know that these are simply judgments that are good to move past. Let your words and resulting feelings simply flow. This will help in ways that I can't describe with words. Please give yourself this gift.

Know that you are loved, more than you can ever imagine. Know that joy is yours each and every day; you only need to choose it and revel in the fact that you have everything that you need right now.

Indeed, blessings abound!

Wishing you peace, joy, and love!

In service,

Dedication

To my mom...

Whose light always lit my path and continues to do so today - from the place that one day we will all call "home".

And...thanks for the apple ;-).

January 1

How much richer would your life be if you committed one night a week to call and reconnect with old friends?

Thoughts?

_____

_____

_____

_____

_____

January 2

Right now is always the perfect time.
Carpe diem!

Thoughts?

_____

_____

_____

_____

_____

January 3

Rest assured – you have all you need right now!

Thoughts?

_____

_____

_____

_____

_____

January 4

Challenge = Teacher.

Thoughts?

_____

_____

_____

_____

_____

January 5

If you always fail forward
is it really failing at all?

Thoughts?

_____

_____

_____

_____

_____

January 6

Bless the unknown; as you raise your foot
for your next step, smile knowing that the
path has already been laid.

Thoughts?

_____

_____

_____

_____

_____

January 7

When we get to the point where we can love and not worry about reciprocation, we have experienced true love.

Thoughts?

_____

_____

_____

_____

_____

January 8

Shift judgments to curiosities...
magic will happen!

Thoughts?

_____

_____

_____

_____

_____

January 9

Lessons are a patchwork quilt that becomes
stronger with each thread.

Thoughts?

_____

_____

_____

_____

_____

January 10

Let's start a movement...
serving instead of selling

Thoughts?

_____

_____

_____

_____

_____

January 11

In knowing, there is peace.

Thoughts?

_____

_____

_____

_____

_____

January 12

Seek out the person that challenges you the most.
Bless them, and send them good thoughts.
You'll be amazed at how much they change.

Thoughts?

_____

_____

_____

_____

_____

January 13

Commit a random act of kindness today…
pay it forward.

Are you game?

Thoughts?

_____

_____

_____

_____

January 14

There is never failure if you learn from the
teachers you've been blessed with.

Thoughts?

_____

_____

_____

_____

_____

January 15

You own your life, no one else.
It's time to rise from victim to victor!

Thoughts?

_____

_____

_____

_____

_____

January 16

Worries simply taint what is inherently
beautiful... you!

Thoughts?

_____

_____

_____

_____

_____

January 17

You are the solution to every challenge
you have.

Thoughts?

_____

_____

_____

_____

_____

January 18

He who dies with the most
people served – wins!

Thoughts?

_____

_____

_____

_____

_____

January 19

Here's an awareness exercise – try
(even just for one hour) not to judge anything.
Once we discover how much we judge,
we can change it.

Thoughts?

_____

_____

_____

_____

_____

January 20

To live a life of service is the highest calling.

Thoughts?

_____

_____

_____

_____

_____

January 21

Light the path of others in order to
illuminate your own.

Thoughts?

_____

_____

_____

_____

_____

January 22

We possess a place of inner peace that we
can tap at will. The question is – do you
know where it is?

Thoughts?

_____

_____

_____

_____

_____

January 23

Everything that comes to you is for a reason,
so why worry?

Thoughts?

_____

_____

_____

_____

January 24

If you are ever feeling without, just go quiet
and look within.

Thoughts?

_____

_____

_____

_____

January 25

Joy and fear share the same pathway in your brain.
One cannot exist at the same time as the other.
Which do you choose?

Thoughts?

_____

_____

_____

_____

_____

January 26

The next time you see a so-called flaw in
yourself, simply see it as the opportunity for
growth that it really is.

Thoughts?

_____

_____

_____

_____

_____

January 27

It's not what so-called success you achieve that truly matters, it's what you become.

Thoughts?

_____

_____

_____

_____

_____

January 28

It's amazing how our issues disappear when we help others.

Thoughts?

_____

_____

_____

_____

_____

January 29

Do you put your greatest gifts to work?
A Gallop poll said that 80% of people
never use their greatest gifts.

Thoughts?

_____

_____

_____

_____

_____

January 30

Right at this very moment you are surrounded by
more blessings than you can imagine... rejoice!

Thoughts?

_____

_____

_____

_____

_____

January 31

When we evolve to the point where we give gratitude for all our challenges, incredible things will manifest.

Thoughts?

_____

_____

_____

_____

_____

February 1

When we truly love ourselves, we are able to fully love others.

Thoughts?

_____

_____

_____

_____

_____

February 2

Our lives are a book that has already been
written. The brilliance of the plan is that we
are only given one chapter at a time....

Thoughts?

_____

_____

_____

_____

_____

February 3

There is a teacher in every fall. When we don't
get the lesson, guess what happens again?

Thoughts?

_____

_____

_____

_____

_____

February 4

We, not they, are the only way!

Thoughts?

_____

_____

_____

_____

_____

February 5

When we look to serve others,
we serve ourselves.

Thoughts?

_____

_____

_____

_____

_____

February 6

If you are in a place of gratitude, and I mean
real gratitude, all worries vanish.

Thoughts?

_____

_____

_____

_____

_____

February 7

Worrying only benefits doctors
and morticians.

Thoughts?

_____

_____

_____

_____

_____

February 8

Don't listen to the voice in your head;
listen to the one in your heart.

Thoughts?

_____

_____

_____

_____

_____

February 9

Do you have an accountability partner?
Get one and see what happens....

Thoughts?

_____

_____

_____

_____

_____

February 10

Our wisdom comes from our journey.
Enjoy the lesson today gives you.

Thoughts?

_____

_____

_____

_____

_____

February 11

How would you define success if money
and things didn't count?

Thoughts?

_____

_____

_____

_____

_____

_____

February 12

If we live our lives aligned with our values,
stress evaporates.

Thoughts?

_____

_____

_____

_____

_____

February 13

Once we've found our passion,
we've found our path.

Thoughts?

_____

_____

_____

_____

_____

February 14

Life is a big boomerang.
Whatever you put out there, you get back.

Thoughts?

_____

_____

_____

_____

_____

February 15

When we silence our ego we can tap
into our soul.

Thoughts?

_____

_____

_____

_____

_____

_____

February 16

Every answer lies in stillness.

Thoughts?

_____

_____

_____

_____

February 17

When we give first we always get...
and it's soooo much sweeter.

Thoughts?

_____

_____

_____

_____

_____

February 18

L.O.V.E. – let our values emerge.

Thoughts?

_____

_____

_____

_____

_____

February 19

Bless all who you encounter.
Everyone comes to you for a reason;
it's up to you to discern the lesson.

Thoughts?

_____

_____

_____

_____

_____

February 20

When we are inspired we become conduits
for a greater message.

Thoughts?

_____

_____

_____

_____

_____

February 21

Every challenge only exists between our
ears.

Thoughts?

_____

_____

_____

_____

_____

February 22

Judging only limits our growth.
Accepting bridges all gaps.

Thoughts?

_____

_____

_____

_____

_____

February 23

A life filled with worry is no life at all.

Thoughts?

_____

_____

_____

_____

_____

February 24

Before you get out of bed each morning give thanks for 10 things in your life. You'll be amazed at how it changes your day.

Thoughts?

_____

_____

_____

_____

_____

February 25

Worry is fear: fear created by your ego to separate you from the truth.

Thoughts?

_____

_____

_____

_____

_____

February 26

The only true foe we will ever face
is our own ego.

Thoughts?

_____

_____

_____

_____

_____

February 27

Life is not about falling but getting up.
Which do you focus on?

Thoughts?

_____

_____

_____

_____

_____

February 28

Thank and bless those who challenge you the most. They are our greatest teachers.

Thoughts?

_____

_____

_____

_____

_____

March 1

Know that you have to love yourself before you can truly love another.

Thoughts?

_____

_____

_____

_____

_____

March 2

If you are not trying, are you dying?

Thoughts?

_____

_____

_____

_____

_____

March 3

Values are lived, not spoken.

Thoughts?

_____

_____

_____

_____

_____

March 4

Forgive yourself first... then forgiveness will flow to others.

Thoughts?

_____

_____

_____

_____

_____

March 5

Ask those who you care about the most where they want to fit into your calendar and see what happens.

Thoughts?

_____

_____

_____

_____

_____

March 6

The light within you can cast out every
darkness.

Thoughts?

_____

_____

_____

_____

_____

March 7

Try not to judge anything for just one day;
you'll be amazed what happens.
Oh, and start with yourself.

Thoughts?

_____

_____

_____

_____

_____

March 8

How do you define success?
Think about it for a minute; is it your
definition or someone else's?

Thoughts?

_____

_____

_____

_____

_____

March 9

Would you worry if you knew that everything
that happens in your life is meant to be?

Thoughts?

_____

_____

_____

_____

_____

March 10

Think and thank – think of all the blessings that you have and give thanks for each one of them... every day!

Thoughts?

_____

_____

_____

_____

_____

March 11

Success is only defined by you, no one else.

Thoughts?

_____

_____

_____

_____

_____

March 12

What if we viewed every fall as a learning opportunity? Think how that would change your perception of your hurdles.

Thoughts?

_____

_____

_____

_____

_____

March 13

Living in service to others
is the highest calling.

Thoughts?

_____

_____

_____

_____

_____

March 14

Take a few minutes today and write down
all that is worrying you. After you get
everything down on paper – tear it up.
Free yourself!

Thoughts?

_____

_____

_____

_____

_____

March 15

Trust in the fact that your path in life is the
ideal one and all your worries will evaporate.

Thoughts?

_____

_____

_____

_____

_____

March 16

In giving, we get. It's all a big boomerang.
What we put out there, we get back.

Thoughts?

_____

_____

_____

_____

_____

March 17

The greatest thing we can do while we are on
this earth is to serve others.

Thoughts?

_____

_____

_____

_____

_____

March 18

List 10 things you are grateful for before
you get out of bed each morning. You'll be
amazed at how your day brightens.

Thoughts?

_____

_____

_____

_____

_____

March 19

Act as if all your desires were coming true...
right now (because they are)!

Thoughts?

_____

_____

_____

_____

_____

March 20

Every day is a clean palette upon which you
can paint your life's story.

Thoughts?

_____

_____

_____

_____

_____

March 21

When you look in the mirror see the person
you want to be. Guess what will happen?

Thoughts?

_____

_____

_____

_____

_____

March 22

There's a reason there aren't luggage racks on a hearse.

Thoughts?

_____

_____

_____

_____

_____

March 23

Please know that right now you are in the exact place that you need to be.

Thoughts?

_____

_____

_____

_____

_____

March 24

If I see the beauty in nature don't I see the beauty in me?

Thoughts?

_____

_____

_____

_____

March 25

Success is not an achievement; it's who you become along your journey that really counts.

Thoughts?

_____

_____

_____

_____

_____

March 26

Close your eyes and take three really deep breaths. Repeat this 10 times a day and see what happens.

Thoughts?

_____

_____

_____

_____

_____

March 27

Act as if nothing could go wrong
(because it can't)!

Thoughts?

_____

_____

_____

_____

_____

March 28

The very best way to help yourself is to help someone else.

Thoughts?

_____

_____

_____

_____

_____

March 29

If you are in a place of gratitude, and I mean real gratitude, all your worries will vanish.

Thoughts?

_____

_____

_____

_____

_____

March 30

What would people say at your eulogy?
Live your life from your eulogy backwards!

Thoughts?

_____

_____

_____

_____

_____

March 31

Once we live in gratitude,
more blessings befall us.

Thoughts?

_____

_____

_____

_____

_____

_____

April 1

It takes supreme courage to fail forward.

Thoughts?

_____

_____

_____

_____

_____

April 2

What you do is not who you are.

Thoughts?

_____

_____

_____

_____

_____

April 3

How would you act if you knew you could never fail?

Thoughts?

_____

_____

_____

_____

_____

April 4

Love every lesson you learn, for each of them builds upon the other.

Thoughts?

_____

_____

_____

_____

_____

April 5

To be of service is to live in spirit.

Thoughts?

_____

_____

_____

_____

April 6

What one thing do you need to focus on today in order to achieve your long-term goals?

Thoughts?

_____

_____

_____

_____

_____

April 7

Love is not a zero sum game.

Thoughts?

_____

_____

_____

_____

_____

April 8

Imagine a life with no worries...
you can make it so!

Thoughts?

_____

_____

_____

_____

_____

April 9

Serving others leads to the greatest success.

Thoughts?

_____

_____

_____

_____

_____

April 10

Imagine being loved unconditionally for who
you really are. Guess what? You are!

Thoughts?

_____

_____

_____

_____

_____

April 11

How may I serve? How may I serve? How may I serve? Four words that can change your life.

Thoughts?

_____

_____

_____

_____

_____

April 12

Act as if you are receiving the exact things you need at all times (because you are)!

Thoughts?

_____

_____

_____

_____

_____

April 13

How we spend our money and
our time reflect our true values.
How do you spend yours?

Thoughts?

_____

_____

_____

_____

_____

April 14

Act as if you are all you need
(because you are)!

Thoughts?

_____

_____

_____

_____

_____

April 15

Your world is simply a reflection of
what is in you.

Thoughts?

_____

_____

_____

_____

_____

April 16

You are all that you ever need... ever!

Thoughts?

_____

_____

_____

_____

_____

April 17

The true you resides in the silence.

Thoughts?

_____

_____

_____

_____

_____

April 18

Love with wild abandon!

Thoughts?

_____

_____

_____

_____

_____

April 19

Rise above the opinion of others;
yours is the only one that matters.

Thoughts?

_____

_____

_____

_____

April 20

Be your own best friend.

Thoughts?

_____

_____

_____

_____

_____

April 21

Let the light in your heart shine in your world.

Thoughts?

_____

_____

_____

_____

April 22

Living in bliss is a choice.

Thoughts?

_____

_____

_____

_____

_____

57

April 23

You are as important as anyone on this planet!

Thoughts?

_____

_____

_____

_____

_____

April 24

The difference your life makes is known to many and appreciated by all.

Thoughts?

_____

_____

_____

_____

_____

_____

April 25

Bloom no matter the season of your life.

Thoughts?

_____

_____

_____

_____

_____

April 26

Care for yourself first so you can care for others.

Thoughts?

_____

_____

_____

_____

_____

April 27

Every single person you encounter has
meaning for you.

Thoughts?

_____

_____

_____

_____

_____

April 28

Give gratitude! Give gratitude!
Give gratitude!

Thoughts?

_____

_____

_____

_____

_____

April 29

Bless those who seem to hurt you the most;
it changes the whole game.

Thoughts?

_____

_____

_____

_____

_____

April 30

Improvement comes from working on things
that irritate us most in others.

Thoughts?

_____

_____

_____

_____

_____

May 1

Acknowledge negative thoughts; bless them and send them on their way. Soon their way will not be yours.

Thoughts?

_____

_____

_____

_____

_____

May 2

Worry undermines all.

Thoughts?

_____

_____

_____

_____

_____

May 3

Happiness is a choice... yours.

Thoughts?

_____

_____

_____

_____

_____

May 4

Your energy is reflected in those you see around you.

Thoughts?

_____

_____

_____

_____

_____

May 5

Anger benefits no one.

Thoughts?

_____

_____

_____

_____

May 6

Become an observer of your life.

Thoughts?

_____

_____

_____

_____

_____

May 7

Once you own all that happens in your life
you can change your story.

Thoughts?

_____

_____

_____

_____

_____

May 8

Victims worry and blame others.
Victors own all that is.

Thoughts?

_____

_____

_____

_____

_____

<u>May 9</u>

Your past is not your future.

Thoughts?

_____

_____

_____

_____

_____

<u>May 10</u>

Every so-called adversity is a blessing.

Thoughts?

_____

_____

_____

_____

_____

May 11

You own your life; no one else does.

Thoughts?

_____

_____

_____

_____

_____

May 12

Do the undone; always.

Thoughts?

_____

_____

_____

_____

_____

May 13

Say the unsaid; always.

Thoughts?

_____

_____

_____

_____

_____

May 14

Purity of intention always shines through.

Thoughts?

_____

_____

_____

_____

_____

May 15

Every single moment is a miracle.
Choose to see them as such!

Thoughts?

_____

_____

_____

_____

_____

May 16

Learn to love yourself first.

Thoughts?

_____

_____

_____

_____

_____

May 17

Know that you are absolutely perfect just as
you are.

Thoughts?

_____

_____

_____

_____

_____

May 18

Only own your stuff, no one else's.

Thoughts?

_____

_____

_____

_____

_____

May 19

Look into the mirror and see the light in your eyes; that is your connection to the Source.

Thoughts?

_____

_____

_____

_____

_____

May 20

Take a few minutes each day to sit quietly and gaze upon anything in nature; feel the connection and oneness that is.

Thoughts?

_____

_____

_____

_____

_____

May 21

"I am...." Complete this and repeat it many times a day;   it will become so.

Thoughts?

_____

_____

_____

_____

_____

May 22

Peace is the ultimate goal...
for everyone and everything.

Thoughts?

_____

_____

_____

_____

_____

May 23

Hover above your life every day... see it
objectively and bless it for all that it is.

Thoughts?

_____

_____

_____

_____

_____

May 24

In every conversation, send blessings and
good thoughts to whomever you are speaking
with; miracles will ensue.

Thoughts?

_____

_____

_____

_____

_____

May 25

No matter what, you are loved.

Thoughts?

_____

_____

_____

_____

_____

May 26

Things don't happen to you...
they happen for you.

Thoughts?

_____

_____

_____

_____

_____

May 27

All is well... always.

Thoughts?

_____

_____

_____

_____

_____

May 28

You are from the Divine and therefore are Divine. Embrace this and give yourself the love you deserve!

Thoughts?

_____

_____

_____

_____

_____

May 29

How much richer would your life be if you committed one night a week to call and reconnect with old friends?

Thoughts?

_____

_____

_____

_____

_____

May 30

Bless the unknown; as you raise your foot for your next step, smile, knowing that the path has already been laid.

Thoughts?

_____

_____

_____

_____

_____

May 31

How are you better today than you
were yesterday?

Thoughts?

_____

_____

_____

_____

_____

June 1

If we invest in people, profits will come.
If we only focus on profits, people will go.

Thoughts?

_____

_____

_____

_____

_____

June 2

Imagine how your life would change if you moved forward knowing that all things happen FOR YOU, not TO YOU... and I mean ALL things. Hmmm....

Thoughts?

_____

_____

_____

_____

_____

June 3

Remember, bliss is only a breath away....

Thoughts?

_____

_____

_____

_____

_____

June 4

There are never any wrong turns...
only unexpected and beautiful journeys.

Thoughts?

_____

_____

_____

_____

_____

June 5

What will you do today to make a positive
difference for someone?

Thoughts?

_____

_____

_____

_____

_____

June 6

When we help our brothers and sisters,
we help ourselves.

Thoughts?

_____

_____

_____

_____

_____

June 7

Wounds = Wisdom

Thoughts?

_____

_____

_____

_____

_____

June 8

Try listening with only one intention: to absorb what is being said, not what your response will be.

Thoughts?

_____

_____

_____

_____

_____

June 9

What was the last thing that made your heart sing? Give yourself that gift again.

Thoughts?

_____

_____

_____

_____

_____

June 10

Only you control how you feel.
No one makes you feel anything.

Thoughts?

_____

_____

_____

_____

_____

June 11

All you have is the now;
that will never change.

Thoughts?

_____

_____

_____

_____

_____

June 12

Your life is simply a reflection of what you are putting out into the world.

Thoughts?

_____

_____

_____

_____

_____

June 13

All external things reflect how you view yourself.

Thoughts?

_____

_____

_____

_____

_____

June 14

You have ultimate control of everything...
and it starts with your thoughts.

Thoughts?

_____

_____

_____

_____

_____

June 15

You are connected to absolutely everything
you encounter.

Thoughts?

_____

_____

_____

_____

_____

June 16

When you get to the point where you can truly visualize that you have something in your possession, it will appear.

Thoughts?

_____

_____

_____

_____

_____

June 17

You are deserving.

Thoughts?

_____

_____

_____

_____

_____

June 18

You are exactly who you are meant to be.

Thoughts?

_____

_____

_____

_____

_____

June 19

You are the Divine in the flesh.

Thoughts?

_____

_____

_____

_____

_____

June 20

The length of your total journey is up to you.

Thoughts?

_____

_____

_____

_____

_____

June 21

What one thing do you need to let go
of right now?

Thoughts?

_____

_____

_____

_____

_____

June 22

What one person do you need to exit from your life right now?

Thoughts?

_____

_____

_____

_____

_____

June 23

One person's negativity is not yours.
They own it, not you.

Thoughts?

_____

_____

_____

_____

_____

June 24

The unknown is simply a wonderful gift
waiting to be unwrapped.

Thoughts?

_____

_____

_____

_____

_____

June 25

Approach every member of your family as a
soul who's journey you are here to assist with.

Thoughts?

_____

_____

_____

_____

_____

June 26

Allow things to happen for you.

Thoughts?

_____

_____

_____

_____

_____

June 27

Be open to receiving.

Thoughts?

_____

_____

_____

_____

_____

June 28

Kindness is akin to giving yourself a gift.

Thoughts?

_____

_____

_____

_____

June 29

Joy is a choice.

Thoughts?

_____

_____

_____

_____

_____

June 30

Peace is a choice.

Thoughts?

_____

_____

_____

_____

_____

July 1

Love is a choice.

Thoughts?

_____

_____

_____

_____

_____

July 2

Accepting others as they are leads to
accepting ourselves.

Thoughts?

_____

_____

_____

_____

_____

July 3

The most important thing you own is your
own transformation.

Thoughts?

_____

_____

_____

_____

_____

July 4

Judging is only a reflection of who you choose to be.

Thoughts?

_____

_____

_____

_____

_____

July 5

Helping someone else always raises your stature.

Thoughts?

_____

_____

_____

_____

_____

July 6

Tell yourself a few times each day –
"I love you!" – See what happens.

Thoughts?

_____

_____

_____

_____

_____

July 7

Approach each day with wide-eyed wonder;
Miracles will start to reveal themselves.

Thoughts?

_____

_____

_____

_____

_____

July 8

When you find a reason to be grateful
for every single thing in your life, magic will
happen.

Thoughts?

_____

_____

_____

_____

_____

June 9

Be the relative, friend, and spouse you have
always dreamed of... and your dreams will
come true.

Thoughts?

_____

_____

_____

_____

_____

July 10

Your soul will always provide you with the guidance you need. You will only hear its voice in the silence.

Thoughts?

_____

_____

_____

_____

_____

July 11

Intuition is your soul sending you a text message.

Thoughts?

_____

_____

_____

_____

July 12

A smile is a beam of light that illuminates others.

Thoughts?

_____

_____

_____

_____

_____

July 13

Say "I'm open to receiving" a few times each day, and then you'll start receiving.

Thoughts?

_____

_____

_____

_____

_____

July 14

No possession is really yours.

Thoughts?

_____

_____

_____

_____

_____

July 15

Before you go to sleep tonight, give thanks for three things in your life; they will multiply as you sleep.

Thoughts?

_____

_____

_____

_____

_____

July 16

Three deep breaths will bring you more
peace than any substance.

Thoughts?

_____

_____

_____

_____

_____

July 17

Happiness is waiting for you in every
moment. Choose it!

Thoughts?

_____

_____

_____

_____

_____

July 18

Live in awe of each person you encounter
for you know not what they have been
chosen to do.

Thoughts?

_____

_____

_____

_____

July 19

Cry as you need to... smile as you want to...
and laugh out loud more than you think you
should. Like right now!

Thoughts?

_____

_____

_____

_____

_____

July 20

Be the listener you would cherish to hear your own words.

Thoughts?

_____

_____

_____

_____

_____

July 21

Every encounter you have with a person is your chance to change their lives for the better.

Thoughts?

_____

_____

_____

_____

_____

July 22

Be the catalyst for positive change...
starting with your own.

Thoughts?

_____

_____

_____

_____

July 23

Change yourself first.
That is what will change the world.

Thoughts?

_____

_____

_____

_____

_____

July 24

Grace... simply live it.

Thoughts?

_____

_____

_____

_____

_____

July 25

Any opinion is simply a judgment.

Thoughts?

_____

_____

_____

_____

_____

July 26

Send blessings and good thoughts to everyone you encounter. You will be a life magnet for goodness.

Thoughts?

_____

_____

_____

_____

_____

July 27

Hang out with people who bring out the best energy in you, and no one else.

Thoughts?

_____

_____

_____

_____

_____

July 28

Ask someone today how you might
best serve them.

Thoughts?

_____

_____

_____

_____

_____

July 29

You have already changed many lives for the
better just by being who you are.

Thoughts?

_____

_____

_____

_____

_____

July 30

The gifts you have been blessed with create a duty for you to share.

Thoughts?

_____

_____

_____

_____

July 31

You will always be surrounded by love. How does that feel?

Thoughts?

_____

_____

_____

_____

_____

August 1

Your "place" in life is only an observation
from others. All that matters is
what you think.

Thoughts?

_____

_____

_____

_____

_____

August 2

Status is a fabrication by those who have
not discovered how we are truly measured.

Thoughts?

_____

_____

_____

_____

_____

August 3

What others think is simply that....

Thoughts?

_____

_____

_____

_____

_____

August 4

Seek to "know" all that you speak.

Thoughts?

_____

_____

_____

_____

_____

August 5

Say all that you need to say to those you love... you know not when their journey ends.

Thoughts?

_____

_____

_____

_____

_____

August 6

A person's journey is for them to live, not anyone else.

Thoughts?

_____

_____

_____

_____

_____

August 7

When you seek to control it reveals
your fears.

Thoughts?

_____

_____

_____

_____

_____

August 8

Trusting is the greatest act of courage.

Thoughts?

_____

_____

_____

_____

_____

August 9

Remove the word "but" from your vocabulary.

Thoughts?

_____

_____

_____

_____

_____

August 10

Seek to have only observations and
no responses for just one day and
see what happens.

Thoughts?

_____

_____

_____

_____

_____

August 11

Emotionally-charged conversations only lead to words falling on deaf ears.

Thoughts?

_____

_____

_____

_____

_____

August 12

There is no need to fight... ever.

Thoughts?

_____

_____

_____

_____

_____

August 13

Disagreements only reflect an unwillingness
to suspend judgments.

Thoughts?

_____

_____

_____

_____

_____

August 14

Love is not present in any argument.

Thoughts?

_____

_____

_____

_____

_____

August 15

All disagreements are about ourselves...
no one else.

Thoughts?

_____

_____

_____

_____

_____

August 16

Only observe without curiosity.

Thoughts?

_____

_____

_____

_____

_____

August 17

Hover above any challenge in your life.
See how you've created it and then
see how you can solve it.

Thoughts?

_____

_____

_____

_____

_____

August 18

When you fully realize that you created
everything in your life, you will see that the power
that created it has the power to change it.

Thoughts?

_____

_____

_____

_____

_____

August 19

Make every decision with the good of the world in mind.

Thoughts?

_____

_____

_____

_____

_____

August 20

Selfishness is only fear turned outward.

Thoughts?

_____

_____

_____

_____

_____

August 21

The only scarcity that exists is in your
belief that there is any.

Thoughts?

_____

_____

_____

_____

_____

August 22

All of your thoughts are energy...
use them wisely.

Thoughts?

_____

_____

_____

_____

_____

August 23

Pay everything forward...
starting with your thoughts.

Thoughts?

_____

_____

_____

_____

_____

August 24

Enlightenment is a choice... you can either
choose it now or when you pass on to your
next journey.

Thoughts?

_____

_____

_____

_____

_____

August 25

Never underestimate your impact on
the world.

Thoughts?

_____

_____

_____

_____

_____

August 26

The most important advances on this planet
never make the papers.

Thoughts?

_____

_____

_____

_____

_____

August 27

Most of those that we revere reflect the
collective work we need to do.

Thoughts?

_____

_____

_____

_____

_____

August 28

Our revolution depends on harnessing
our thoughts.

Thoughts?

_____

_____

_____

_____

_____

August 29

We don't need to learn to love our enemies...
we need   to learn that we have no enemies.

Thoughts?

_____

_____

_____

_____

_____

August 30

If you only knew how many people you
inspire each day....

Thoughts?

_____

_____

_____

_____

_____

August 31

If you wish to make an impact on this planet
simply always lead the way with love.

Thoughts?

_____

_____

_____

_____

_____

September 1

Inspiration is a direct line to the Divine.

Thoughts?

_____

_____

_____

_____

_____

September 2

The greatest love story is the ore you
should have with yourself.

Thoughts?

_____

_____

_____

_____

_____

September 3

I am....

Thoughts?

_____

_____

_____

_____

_____

September 4

You were sent here with a purpose and all that you need to accomplish your goals.

Thoughts?

_____

_____

_____

_____

_____

September 5

Your success is gauged by a force much higher than any on this earth.

Thoughts?

_____

_____

_____

_____

_____

September 6

Inspired action leads to otherworldly results.

Thoughts?

_____

_____

_____

_____

_____

September 7

Care for yourself as you would for someone whom you cherish.

Thoughts?

_____

_____

_____

_____

_____

September 8

Living gracefully is what you are meant to do.

Thoughts?

_____

_____

_____

_____

_____

September 9

Every morning rise knowing that
your #1 goal is to be joyful.

Thoughts?

_____

_____

_____

_____

_____

September 10

Seek to be in a place of gratitude...
where you see the miracle of each breath.

Thoughts?

_____

_____

_____

_____

_____

September 11

No one has ever, or will ever,
be a better you than you.

Thoughts?

_____

_____

_____

_____

_____

September 12

Celebrate everything that is unique
about yourself.

Thoughts?

_____

_____

_____

_____

_____

September 13

Silence... Silence... Silence.

Thoughts?

_____

_____

_____

_____

_____

September 14

Take five minutes today to act like
a five-year-old.

Thoughts?

_____

_____

_____

_____

_____

September 15

Remember that children are closer to our
Source because they were just there.

Thoughts?

_____

_____

_____

_____

_____

September 16

Seek to remember the great forgotten...
where we come from.

Thoughts?

_____

_____

_____

_____

September 17

Your journey was your choice.
Embrace this and let joy emerge.

Thoughts?

_____

_____

_____

_____

_____

September 18

What if every person you saw that was so-called disabled, ill, or homeless was a more evolved soul with a higher calling? How would that change things for you?

Thoughts?

_____

_____

_____

_____

September 19

Act as if we have no borders, politics, or religion.

Thoughts?

_____

_____

_____

_____

_____

September 20

Your voice deserves to be heard just as
much as any other.

Thoughts?

_____

_____

_____

_____

September 21

You are grace.

Thoughts?

_____

_____

_____

_____

_____

September 22

True peace resides within.

Thoughts?

_____

_____

_____

_____

_____

September 23

You ARE love, and deserve to BE loved.

Thoughts?

_____

_____

_____

_____

_____

September 24

Hug as many people as you can.

Thoughts?

_____

_____

_____

_____

_____

September 25

Leave no doubt with those whom you love.

Thoughts?

_____

_____

_____

_____

_____

September 26

When in doubt, express yourself.

Thoughts?

_____

_____

_____

_____

_____

September 27

Use words that are beautiful; as beautiful as the silence that they interrupt.

Thoughts?

_____

_____

_____

_____

_____

September 28

Pointing out our differences serves only to
create a divide between us.

Thoughts?

_____

_____

_____

_____

September 29

Seek to emphasize what binds us together.

Thoughts?

_____

_____

_____

_____

_____

September 30

When you realize you are the only solution,
the world will change.

Thoughts?

_____

_____

_____

_____

_____

October 1

Embrace the fact that your thoughts can
change the world.

Thoughts?

_____

_____

_____

_____

_____

October 2

Your physical body is not who you really are.

Thoughts?

_____

_____

_____

_____

_____

October 3

You have 60,000 thoughts each day...
use them wisely.

Thoughts?

_____

_____

_____

_____

_____

October 4

71% of your thoughts are negative... hmmm....

Thoughts?

_____

_____

_____

_____

_____

October 5

95% of your thoughts are the same ones you had yesterday... hmmm....

Thoughts?

_____

_____

_____

_____

_____

October 6

And the key to change is what?

Thoughts?

_____

_____

_____

_____

_____

October 7

Be clear about what you desire and believe that it is already here.

Thoughts?

_____

_____

_____

_____

_____

October 8

Your ego tries to make you believe you
can't... know that you can.

Thoughts?

_____

_____

_____

_____

_____

October 9

Your ego is your less-evolved self trying to
hold on to the past.

Thoughts?

_____

_____

_____

_____

_____

October 10

Every time you look back it hinders your ability to get ahead.

Thoughts?

_____

_____

_____

_____

_____

October 11

There are no secrets or mysteries, only rediscoveries.

Thoughts?

_____

_____

_____

_____

_____

October 12

At birth you knew exactly why you chose to come here. You spend your entire life trying to rediscover what you've always known.

Thoughts?

_____

_____

_____

_____

_____

October 13

Be open to all that happens; once you embrace the uncertainty, allowing begins.

Thoughts?

_____

_____

_____

_____

_____

October 14

The Law of Attraction is simply living
aligned with what is.

Thoughts?

_____

_____

_____

_____

_____

October 15

Talk to people – not about them.

Thoughts?

_____

_____

_____

_____

_____

October 16

How would it feel to have all the power you need right now? Rejoice; you do!

Thoughts?

_____

_____

_____

_____

_____

October 17

Others' opinions of you are a reflection of where they are, not you.

Thoughts?

_____

_____

_____

_____

_____

October 18

Your message has only been given to you;
imagine if you don't reveal it....

Thoughts?

_____

_____

_____

_____

_____

October 19

Understanding is a huge act of love.

Thoughts?

_____

_____

_____

_____

_____

October 20

Forgiveness is love, is action.

Thoughts?

_____

_____

_____

_____

_____

October 21

Forgiveness is only about you...
not what the other person did.

Thoughts?

_____

_____

_____

_____

_____

October 22

Create love... don't wait for it.

Thoughts?

_____

_____

_____

_____

_____

October 23

Love like you can never get hurt;
because you really can't.

Thoughts?

_____

_____

_____

_____

_____

October 24

Life is not a test.

Thoughts?

_____

_____

_____

_____

_____

October 25

You will never be judged by those who matter.

Thoughts?

_____

_____

_____

_____

_____

October 26

Revel in each breath... it is all we really are.

Thoughts?

_____

_____

_____

_____

_____

October 27

Don't let things replace being.

Thoughts?

_____

_____

_____

_____

_____

October 28

Take the leap... you will always grow the
wings when you need them.

Thoughts?

_____

_____

_____

_____

_____

October 29

Stress is just a sign that you are not aligned
with your purpose yet.

Thoughts?

_____

_____

_____

_____

_____

October 30

Busyness is an attempt to cover up the truth.

Thoughts?

_____

_____

_____

_____

_____

October 31

Your internal compass will always find true
north if you open it up.

Thoughts?

_____

_____

_____

_____

_____

November 1

The light you see in your eyes is the gateway to the Source. Look at it often and embrace the connection.

Thoughts?

November 2

What you have done does not reflect what you can become.

Thoughts?

November 3

There is renewal in every breath.

Thoughts?

_____

_____

_____

_____

_____

November 4

Do what makes you feel truly alive.

Thoughts?

_____

_____

_____

_____

_____

November 5

Don't let death come before your heart
stops beating.

Thoughts?

_____

_____

_____

_____

_____

November 6

Pick out one thing today that makes you feel
comfortable... and do it!

Thoughts?

_____

_____

_____

_____

_____

November 7

When you realize that the opinion of others means nothing, you will find freedom.

Thoughts?

_____

_____

_____

_____

_____

November 8

You are not after a career, but a calling.

Thoughts?

_____

_____

_____

_____

_____

November 9

Being comfortable rarely leads to change.

Thoughts?

_____

_____

_____

_____

_____

November 10

Redirect every conversation that is not
steeped in love.

Thoughts?

_____

_____

_____

_____

_____

November 11

Negativity is toxic;
don't expose yourself to it.

Thoughts?

_____

_____

_____

_____

_____

November 12

We can never build a child's self-esteem
enough.

Thoughts?

_____

_____

_____

_____

_____

November 13

Strive to provide five positive comments for every "critique" you offer; it's a game changer.

Thoughts?

_____

_____

_____

_____

_____

November 14

If someone criticizes you, bless them and move on. The ONLY opinion that matters is yours.

Thoughts?

_____

_____

_____

_____

_____

November 15

Intolerance only displays ignorance.

Thoughts?

_____

_____

_____

_____

_____

November 16

Never be intolerant of intolerance.

Thoughts?

_____

_____

_____

_____

_____

November 17

Change comes from taking care of your own
"stuff" first.

Thoughts?

_____

_____

_____

_____

_____

November 18

All the answers we really NEED,
we already have.

Thoughts?

_____

_____

_____

_____

_____

November 19

Give to others like it comes from an endless source... because it does.

Thoughts?

_____

_____

_____

_____

_____

November 20

There is a loop of giving and receiving; be open to letting others help you so that the loop is never-ending.

Thoughts?

_____

_____

_____

_____

_____

November 21

Serotonin is more powerful than
ANY man-made drug.

Thoughts?

_____

_____

_____

_____

_____

November 22

All the healing you need is in your mind
already.

Thoughts?

_____

_____

_____

_____

_____

November 23

The Genesis of all is in nature.

Thoughts?

_____

_____

_____

_____

_____

November 24

Helping others helps you more.

Thoughts?

_____

_____

_____

_____

_____

November 25

Imagine there is a beautiful cord connecting
all of us together... because there is.

Thoughts?

_____

_____

_____

_____

November 26

A person's color is simply God
using his full palette.

Thoughts?

_____

_____

_____

_____

_____

November 27

If we could see a person's chosen journey
when we meet them, we would fall down in
wondrous admiration at their feet.

Thoughts?

_____

_____

_____

_____

November 28

Are you willing to L.O.S.E.?...
Let Our Souls Emerge.

Thoughts?

_____

_____

_____

_____

November 29

Vulnerability is a sign of supreme strength.

Thoughts?

_____

_____

_____

_____

_____

November 30

The only language that really matters
has no words.

Thoughts?

_____

_____

_____

_____

_____

December 1

You are Source. How empowering is that?!

Thoughts?

_____

_____

_____

_____

_____

December 2

Awareness is one of the most powerful tools at your disposal.

Thoughts?

_____

_____

_____

_____

_____

December 3

Ownership of all issues brings freedom.

Thoughts?

_____

_____

_____

_____

_____

December 4

Your thoughts are just that, YOURS.
Let them reflect who you really are.

Thoughts?

_____

_____

_____

_____

_____

December 5

The truth forms a layer below your
conscious thoughts.

Thoughts?

_____
_____
_____
_____

December 6

Strive to have 20 minutes of quiet time
each day; it is one of the best gifts
you can give yourself.

Thoughts?

_____
_____
_____
_____

December 7

What if your dreams could create what you see as your reality? Hmmm....

Thoughts?

_____

_____

_____

_____

_____

December 8

Labeling serves no one and harms many.

Thoughts?

_____

_____

_____

_____

_____

December 9

Embracing our so-called differences is one of the BIG lessons we are here to learn.

Thoughts?

_____

_____

_____

_____

_____

December 10

Speak to those that frighten you.

Thoughts?

_____

_____

_____

_____

_____

December 11

Want the key to the city? Simply smile.

Thoughts?

_____

_____

_____

_____

_____

December 12

Your life journey won't be judged,
it will be marveled at!

Thoughts?

_____

_____

_____

_____

_____

December 13

Being in the "flow" is alignment with all that is.

Thoughts?

_____

_____

_____

_____

_____

December 14

Pity no one; simply love them.

Thoughts?

_____

_____

_____

_____

_____

December 15

Make a list of all that scares you – then pick one thing to conquer each week.

Thoughts?

_____

_____

_____

_____

_____

December 16

In each death is renewal... for those departed, and for those remaining.

Thoughts?

_____

_____

_____

_____

_____

December 17

Internal peace starts with a love of yourself.

Thoughts?

_____

_____

_____

_____

December 18

Trusting is the best gift you can give
yourself.

Thoughts?

_____

_____

_____

_____

_____

December 19

Don't work hard... learn to just let things flow.

Thoughts?

_____

_____

_____

_____

_____

December 20

Wisdom is never possessed...
it is simply passed on.

Thoughts?

_____

_____

_____

_____

_____

178

December 21

Forgiveness unlocks your true self.

Thoughts?

_____

_____

_____

_____

_____

December 22

Receiving is just as important as giving.

Thoughts?

_____

_____

_____

_____

_____

December 23

Letting a person help you is one of the
greatest gifts you can give them.

Thoughts?

_____

_____

_____

_____

_____

December 24

How would you act and feel if you knew you
were perfect in every way? Well... you are.

Thoughts?

_____

_____

_____

_____

_____

December 25

Power is fear. Perfectionism is judging.
Striving is ego. And you don't need to
employ any of these.

Thoughts?

_____

_____

_____

_____

_____

December 26

The world is your mirror.

Thoughts?

_____

_____

_____

_____

_____

December 27

Believing others more than yourself is giving away what you have been blessed with.

Thoughts?

_____

_____

_____

_____

_____

December 28

Thinking and feeling always take a back seat to knowing.

Thoughts?

_____

_____

_____

_____

_____

December 29

The universe resides in you.

Thoughts?

_____

_____

_____

_____

_____

December 30

Life is meant to be about Peace, Joy, and Love.

Thoughts?

_____

_____

_____

_____

_____

December 31

If you learn to forgive,
you have lived your purpose.

Thoughts?

_____

_____

_____

_____

_____

About Drayton

<u>A. Drayton Boylston</u> is the Founder and CEO of the <u>Boylston Group of Companies</u> which include: <u>The Rescue Institute</u>, <u>The Executive Coaching University</u>, and <u>CareerTrainingPrograms.com</u>. The overarching mission of this collective group of companies is to help 10 million people *save themselves from the lives they've created!* ®

He is a pioneer in the field of Executive Coaching and is considered a Leadership Visionary. He considers himself, first and foremost, a Servant Leader.

He is the author of <u>Coming UnScrooged</u>™- a highly acclaimed book on corporate rescue and redemption.

His companies have trained thousands of people in 36 countries around the world in personal leadership and coaching skills. His Executive Coaching University is widely considered to be one of the leading Coach Training and Personal Development firms in the world.

All of their work is values-based. The goal is to help individuals and organizations lead based upon their core values, focusing on their most important asset- their people.

Their core belief is that Coaching is the Cure for This Crisis! ™

Drayton can be reached at
Drayton@RescueInstitute.org or 1.800.251.1696.

Media and speaking inquiries please visit:
http://www.rescueinstitute.org/ri-media-page

Resources

The Personal Greatness Program:
www.PersonalGreatness.com

The Executive Coaching University:
www.ExecutiveCoachingUniversity.com/

Executive Coaching and Mentoring:
www.TheBoylstonGroup.com

1.800.251.1696

Please visit:
www.ExecutiveCoachingUniversity.com/

to learn more about:

- Courses and Teleclasses
- Seminars and Workshops
- Coaching and Mentoring

www.ingramcontent.com/pod-product-compliance
Lightning Source LLC
LaVergne TN
LVHW051517080426
835509LV00017B/2086